IT'S A GOOD DAY TO DIE

SOME PERSONAL POETRY ABOUT
THE UPS AND DOWNS IN MY LIFE

JAY THOMAS WILLIS

IT'S A GOOD DAY TO DIE
SOME PERSONAL POETRY ABOUT THE UPS AND DOWNS IN MY LIFE

iUniverse books may be ordered through booksellers or by contacting:

iUniverse
1663 Liberty Drive
Bloomington, IN 47403
www.iuniverse.com
1-800-Authors (1-800-288-4677)

ISBN: 978-1-5320-9885-7 (sc)
ISBN: 978-1-5320-9886-4 (e)

Library of Congress Control Number: 2020908512

Print information available on the last page.

iUniverse rev. date: 05/15/2020

DEDICATION

This book of poems is dedicated to Crazy Horse, and other Native Americans, for their immortal words, "It's a good day to die." Historically, these words were credited to Crazy Horse, but were known to have been uttered by any number of Native Americans as they prepared to engage in battle. These words became a mantra for the Native Americans.

Anytime a single person or a group tries to move in on you, lock, stock and barrel; then, "It's a good day to die," as Crazy Horse, Low Dog, and other Native Americans cried out when about to engage in war….

CONTENTS

PART II - LIFE IN GENERAL

PART III - FAMILY

PART IV - THE ENVIRONMENT

PART V - PERSONAL ISSUES

PART VI - EDUCATION

ACKNOWLEDGMENTS

Thanks to the indomitable spirit of Crazy Horse and other Native Americans. May their spirit live on in the hearts and minds of the American and Native American people.

Thanks to the Almighty God for giving me a rich variety of life experiences.

ALSO BY JAY THOMAS WILLIS

AUTHOR'S NOTE

I was born in East Texas. Went to elementary, junior high, and high school there; later attended college at a nearby institution. I then joined the military: spending time in Orlando, Florida; Chicago, Illinois; and Chelsea, Massachusetts. Matriculated graduate school in Houston, Texas, and later moved to a South Suburb of Chicago. I have lived there for the past forty-six years.

"It's a good day to die" is a phrase historically associated with Native American cultures, but its actual origin is unclear. There seems to be a lot of confusion about where the phrase actually originated from; it is believed that the phrase did originate with the Native Americans. The phrase has also been associated with other cultures.

Although, the phrase has historically been attributed to Crazy Horse as he began to engage in the battle of Little Big Horn. Also, Low Dog, one of Sitting Bull's men was known to have uttered the phrase, *this is a good day to die.* The Indians felt they should be ready to die on any given day and have no regrets. That's why they felt it was important to begin each day fresh, and not let past problems or present distractions cloud how God wants us to live.

I portray the good, bad, ugly, and significant events in my life. Moving from childhood in East Texas (elementary, junior high, and high school), to college, to the military, and through the latter parts of my life in Chicago.

Life has been good, but there have also been some rough spots. Narrowly escaping the jaws of death on a number of occasions, but have always come out in good form. Knowing death is always lurking just around the corner, hiding in the shadows.

Through my poetry I portray some of these scenarios. I am not a seasoned poet, but decided it was time to write a book of poetry, and felt the need to express myself in that genre. I hope all those who pick up this book of poetry will find it acceptable and enjoyable.

Because of the instability in my life, I have always considered any day to be a good day to die. Knowing that a continuous life is not guaranteed to anyone. I felt that in view of this fact the chosen title was a good one for this book of poetry.

Although, I don't believe that because I consider any day to be a good day to die that one should live their lives in a reckless manner; but should have reverence for all human life, and should treat all people with respect and dignity.

Freud elaborates on the concepts of Eros and Thanatos: Eros being the life instinct, and Thanatos the death instinct. These are two fundamental drives of life. Some people are motivated to live, primarily; and some people are motivated to die, primarily. It is felt that most people are motivated to live; but under pressure, will reluctantly accept death. Beneath the surface for most people, *it's always a good day to die.*

This book consists of a series of poems about the ups and downs in my life. The poetry in this book was born from struggle, war, trials, tribulations, and storms. I fundamentally believe that we must all be prepared to die any day.

PART 1

LOVE INTEREST

AN UNREQUITED LOVE

I never did meet Laura, but I admired her from afar, she was a star. She lived in the projects; around the corner from my father's street inlet.

She was five-two and mature for her age; upon seeing her I exploded in a rage. She had nice buttocks, hips, and legs; at thirteen I dreamed of getting her in bed.

I would sit near the window and watch her as she went by on her way to the store; I only wished I could see her more. I never did say anything to her; didn't have enough nerve. For me my confidence didn't serve.

I was hoping to have more confidence another day, but the next year, my friend told me she had moved away. I would go into the projects to see if I could get a better look, and end up running away, using all the energy it took.

ALYALA

Alyala was a pretty girl; how much I wanted to be in her world. She was tall and slender, but I had high hopes she would surrender.

She weighed about 120 lbs., with long-black-straight hair, built like a brick shithouse, as they say in certain parts of the South. In addition, she had a pretty face, perfectly formed body, and well-shaped legs.

She was a few years ahead of me, and I knew what I wanted could never be. She had two much style, class, and savoir-faire. I hadn't been around anywhere.

All I knew was the sticks, and was just a tie-tongued prick. She graduated and went her own way. I kept wishing there was some way she could stay.

I saw her for the last time at her graduation. I knew that would be the secession. I found out later that she was a close cousin on both sides of the clan, and that I would just have to grow up and be a man.

CHERRIE

I thought Cherrie was special. She had big hips, a pretty face, and dressed in lace. She had big breast and smooth legs that made me want to get on my knees and beg.

She was built for performance, especially romance. She had long-black hair and yellow skin; the kind a lot of people loved to get in.

But I wasn't ready for romance, and would barely get a chance. She put up with me for a while, but I felt deep down inside that she didn't like my style.

She rejected me many times; until, I found myself in a bind. I could either keep being her fool or take her to school.

After so much neglect I started to reflect. So, we quit, and I split. I had some definite plans of my own, I wasn't a child, I was damn near grown.

So, I forgot her and went to college, trying to get some of that book knowledge. If she had pressured me, I would have married her on the spot. I was in love and would have danced on a dot.

But she didn't care, and she was just having fun. As far as she was concerned it should have long ago been done. So, I went away and never looked back. Kept moving with my pack.

I never came back on a white horse or a silver cloud to rescue her, for that I'm happy to demure.

THE PRETTIEST GIRL

I met her in a department store, and wanted to see more. She was a sales girl, and one of the prettiest in the world. I hadn't been around much, and had little to compare her to, but I wanted her to be my boo.

She had smooth, round, well-formed legs; nice breast; well-managed hair; an overall-nice body; and a pretty face—she brightened up the place. She had a pleasant personality, was agreeable, and amenable; she wasn't like some girls who made you feel tenable.

Every time I saw her, she looked immaculate, clean, and fresh—I thought she was the best. She was always in my dreams, and schemes, but I was only a boy with few viable and constructive means.

I came back to the store whenever I had a few dollars to buy anything. I bought things I didn't want or need, just to get a look at her—if you please.

I know she never had toward me any personal intentions, if she did, she failed to mention them. If she wanted to get to know me, she had plenty of time to show me.

I wanted to ask her out, but at the time had too much doubt. The time came when I would come in the store but didn't see her any more.

I supposed the Almighty God had closed that door. I still think of her now and again, but you can't get back what never could have been.

MY FAVORITE STORE

I got in the habit of buying designer clothes—even in high school I only shopped in specialty stores; not Sanctuary Place, Suns, or Cross. These were usually the only stores to explore.

One day I walked into my favorite place, and purchased a few things, and the young lady told me I had excellent taste. She told me if I wasn't doing anything at seven to come by her place.

She said she was a college student, and working her way through college, while trying to obtain some necessary knowledge.

I went by her place at seven and found holy heaven. I went by on several occasions, but must have lost my persuasion. She left after a year, and moved back to New York, said she was tired of the small-town retort.

I never saw her again, was I asking too much, because I wanted her to be my friend. I hope I run into her before the end.

FOR MY BELOVED SHELLY

Shelly was built like a Shetland pony. I wanted her to be my tender roni. I met her in biology class and wanted our relationship to last. She was five-two, with huge buttocks, the kind that most men would flock. She would strut and prance like a game cock; it made my heart rock.

I went by her dorm to see her several times, but our chemistry didn't rhyme. I was nervous and jittery like a coyote, and couldn't take note. I saw her on any number of occasions, but she didn't feel I was of the right persuasion. She eventually left the university; said she was looking for more diversity.

I never saw her again. Last time I saw her she said she was tired of make-believe and pretend.

ALYSSIA

Of all the girls I never dated, Alyssia was the highest rated. For some reason we never got together; the reason is floating in the weather.

For some reason I never paid her much attention; even though she was pretty and would at times bring me to her mention.

After high school I realized I had made a serious mistake; only to realize at that point it was too late.

I got one more chance, but blew that on a gambled romance. I had no foresight, couldn't be upright.

Sorry we didn't get together earlier in our lives, and that I didn't keep my eyes on the special prize.

KADIYA

Kadiya was a sweet and pretty thing; the kind you'd want to give your ring. She was smooth and well bred, and she also had a good head.

I met her in the Niki Burger; while also looking for a love merger. She was smooth and lean; you know the college girl type, I couldn't even come up with a gripe.

She was friendly and open to a relationship; she accidently let that slip. I walked her to her dorm; I didn't think that would do any harm.

We saw each other for a while, but eventually decided we had absolutely different styles. After a week I saw her with someone new; I would live to regret that moment too.

Even today, I think about Kadiya, and how good it could have been. If only our minds could have handled the trend.

A PERFECT TEN

While in college, I opened an account at the city college bank. I walked in and she immediately caught my eye.

She was slender and trim with nice legs, breast, and buttocks. She had a well-managed coiffeur and a pretty face.

I knew I was there for a particular reason and could not dally; though, I wished I could meet her. But what would she want with a plain-John like me?

But as they say, "sometimes there's no accounting for taste." I came back to the bank on several occasions, but never did chance to meet her—to my dismay.

She ran through my mind and through my dreams until she ran completely out of them.

BE CAREFUL WHAT
YOU WISH FOR

I didn't get what I wished for but came close enough.

While in college, I frequented a college bar, always looking for a star. I met a young lady who was 34-28-36, a pretty face, nice legs and breast, a cool demeanor, and she was the prettiest lady I had ever seen by far.

I got her phone number and asked if she lived alone. She said call and come over some time; she must have known what was on my Mind.

I called the next day, and she examined her little black book and said she was free, just waiting for only me. Come about eight tomorrow night, and don't be late.

As soon as I got in the room, I felt doom and gloom. She had two German shepherds and two Siamese cats, said she was a college brat, and hadn't had time to clean.

My nose was incensed even though I was no prince. The place was filthy, dirty, and nasty; as you might expect with rare cleanings, two dogs, and two cats.

She said she was working her way through college while taking seventeen semester hours. We talked for a while until I couldn't stand the smell. I was going through hell. I quickly decided this was not within my power.

I didn't get what I wished for but came close. be careful you don't get a dose of what you yearn for.

FOR MY BELOVED SUSAN

Susan was the perfect girl for me. She was young, tender, and five-feet-three. One day we were both sitting in history class; I couldn't wait for the hour to pass.

I wanted to ask her what was her name, and if I could play her game. After class, I saw her on the way out, she was waiting for me, as if I had tremendous clout.

She also had lovely legs, breast, and buttocks; the kind that would make any man stop. She also had nice hair, character, and personality to spare.

She invited me to her off-campus apartment, and said it would lead to both our betterment. We had wine and engage in some good times.

I went by her apartment for the rest of my time at the university; said she was pleased to find someone trustworthy.

We both graduated and moved on; said she had to find a new "king-on-the-throne." Said she was from Boston, but was relocating to Austin.

I called her in Austin several years later. She had married and was living larger and greater. After that, I lost contact, and figured there was no comeback.

ODE TO CARRIE

I met Carrie at an urban mall; said she had time to stall. She was five-seven, with a perfect body, and love to folly.

We got a room at a local motel; she said that was swell. We spent the night; she was out-of-sight. I woke up to get a good look, and found her rambling through my pocketbook.

She asked me for my number the next morning before we left the motel, but I thought that would be asking for hell.

I didn't give her my number and didn't slumber. I told her I would make the contact, if there was any reason for a comeback.

We said good-bye, and I forgot about her for a while, but I found myself wanting to once again check out her style.

I came back to the urban mall over and over and over again, but never could find my precious friend.

I guess lightening doesn't strike in the same place twice.

SHE'S GOT LEGS

I met her at one of the fancy-large urban malls. She was fantastic in her personality and character— not at all plastic.

The most apparent thing about her was her beautiful legs. I figured I had to get to know her and move up a peg.

Her legs were hairless, smooth, and perfectly round. That may not sound all that profound.

She was sitting on a bench in sheer pantyhose. I couldn't keep from looking at her legs and toes. I had never seen a pair of legs like that on Such a marvelous creature. I thought it was a perfect feature.

I got her number and went out of my way to make a play for her, but she also didn't like my peculiar purr. Last time I heard she had left town. Took a Job in sales in a town with better sound.

A BRIEF ENCOUNTER

I met her on a Northwestern Illinois train. The way I met her must have given her the idea I was a bit insane. I had my eyes on her from several seats back. I decided to tighten up my act.

I moved closer to her and began a conversation; it was cause for much elation. She launched a big smile and covered her mouth as if she was self-conscious about her braces, but I was only concerned about other places.

As soon as we started talking the conductor yelled out her stop, as if it was a well-planned plot. I was somber and asked for her number. She wrote it and said, "Call me sometimes." I gave her a wide grill and said, "I will."

On a hot and muggy Fourth of July I called to see if I could come by. She said, "Certainly, you can catch me on the fly."

I caught the train, it was the only available transportation, and arrived in the middle of the situation. She lived in a mansion in the better part of the town. The one that I had Little chance to be around.

I stayed for a while, but she saw I was out of place, not that brave soul she wanted to embrace. So, she took me back to the train station and said good-bye, there was more to her situation than met the eye.

She was a student at one of the best Eastern Colleges money could buy. I regret not being able to give her a good try. I never did encounter her again, if nothing else, she would have made a good friend.

CALIFORNIA GIRL

I was in an urban city, lost and out of place, but on the beat. The old saying goes, *stay out of the kitchen if you can't stand the heat.*

I was strolling a local park. All of a sudden, I saw a young lady coming in my direction and smiling at me. She was perfect. Another old saying goes, *be careful what you wish for, you just might get it,* then what will you do with it.

This girl was neat; she was a real treat. I thought the world of her, and voluntarily took myself off the beat. She had everything and made my heart sing.

She said the relationship could last only if I didn't question her about her past. She said she was from a sunshine state, and she had seen the Golden Gate.

We got together often and visited museums, zoos, parks, and theaters. I thought no one was greater. We associated for a while, until her fiancé came to town, and changed our style.

One day she told me her fiancé was coming, and that would be the end of our slumming. She said they had a fight and she only intended to do right. But he was coming for her to get; said they were each other's pet.

I regret losing her to this day, but then I realize there was no other way. Be careful what you wish for, you just might get it, and if you're not careful again, you might lose it.

PART II

LIFE IN GENERAL

A LIGHT AT THE END
OF THE TUNNEL

I've been exposed to tight budgets all my life, but there was a light at the end of the tunnel:

I lived in a house that only used wood as energy; there was no telephone, gas, electricity, or indoor plumbing.

I wore my sister's hand-me-down dresses and pigtails, until I was three years of age, because of my mother's tight budget.

I wore whatever clothing I could get on my tight budget from elementary to high school.

In elementary, junior high, and high school, we had just the basics: no fundamentals of music, no art, and no physical education; to list only a few of the things we didn't have.

I went to an elementary, junior high, and high school that ran on a shoestring budget. There was no daycare, preschool, or kindergarten prior to elementary school.

I just made it through college on my tight budget: I was successful at getting a basic loan. At times I thought I wouldn't make it.

As I left college, I had exhausted all my available funds, and couldn't afford a car or an apartment. The only option I could see for myself at the time was to join the military.

Getting through the military on the basic allotment was of course a Challenge.

After the military I went to graduate school, and found myself on another shoestring budget.

I had been exposed to tight budgets all my life, but once I got a job after graduate school, things did begin to look better, and there was light at the end of the tunnel.

A MILITARY EXPERIENCE

It was in the military that I realized my personality was distorted, and I would have been better off to have been aborted. But no matter what we demand, the Almighty God has His plan. We can plot our whole lives through, but in the end, you get what God has for you.

Some of us went to the enlisted men's club every Friday and Saturday night. We could dance and fraternize; if not we could get involved in a good fight.

I thought I was doing fine until one girl I knew told a friend of mine, "Don't Bring your friend the next time." I didn't know my image was so poor; that I needed to step to the back door.

I never went back to the enlisted men's club again. I went to another city to carry out my sins. I was so ashamed of what the girl had said, but I had made my own bed.

I never felt quite at home, and I always felt for the military, I was wrong.

Maybe for any place!!

BACK HOME IN HOUSTON

After the military, I wanted to be any place but back in the country. I had always heard about Austin, but if I had my way, I would have stayed in Boston.

My folks in the country still lived a primitive existence, that is why in going there, I put up some resistance. They still didn't have a telephone, gas, or indoor plumbing, living there would be like slumming.

I didn't have enough money to live on my own, and I felt like I had been wronged. I stayed with a friend for a while; I did finally figure out his style.

I didn't really want an advanced degree; but It was the only way I could see. I tried the unemployment office, but my friend didn't have a phone, and felt like I was all alone.

One day my friend had some Little Friskies meat patties that were meant for dogs; I had to get out of this bog. He must have considered me lower than a hog.

I figured that was the last straw, and I at that point had to withdraw. I enrolled and moved to the campus of a local college; and once again I was in pursuit of knowledge.

I stayed on campus for a while until I could make other arrangements: participated in campus activities, studied, and made other attainments.

Later, my former roommate asked me to move into an apartment. I thought that was Heaven sent. After obtaining my degree, once again I was free.

I met my wife while visiting at my old *alma mater*. I visited her from that point on at every quarter. She moved to Houston, and we decided to get married, both of us didn't want to further tarry.

We moved to an apartment and got married. All I had was what I could carry. I decided to get another degree; since, unemployment was all I could See.

The government did send me back to school, and furthered my education, but I still lacked a powerful oration.

We did well enough for a while, so we continued to give the marriage a trial.

I graduated and decided I needed to be Re-situated. So, we moved to Chicago, since we couldn't move to Key Largo.

We left in June on a hot afternoon. I was hoping to dance to a new tune. We arrived in Chicago in two days; while hoping to establish some new ways.

JOBS

In my career I went from job to Job. Maintaining a job was incredibly hard. Most people didn't like me, and did things to spite me. Said my personality was not congruent, and I was not affluent.

I thought If I got a college degree, I would have better opportunities. None of my family members had any college, some didn't graduate high school, but they were smooth. Even so, they had a hard time finding a decent job or position, based on my intuition.

The people in my community took what jobs they could find, and I'm not being unkind. I thought if I got a college degree, I would have better opportunities.

I finally got tired of moving from job to job, finding no-holds-barred. So, I gave up looking for that one special job.

LIFE

It's a beautiful place, but no one can win this race. Though, you might have been born in a big old house with an ample supply of butlers and maids.

Life is full of strife, and you can't get out of it alive. It's a zero-sum game; everyone must at times look a little lame.

Everyone has their own share of problems, and it's sometimes difficult to solve them. We get things sometimes taken off the front end and placed on the back bend; the game is rigged to follow a certain trend.

Sometimes our hearts will not mend, yet sometimes we walk around with a silly grin, but this is life and we must endure the sin.

We lose our jobs and our marriages fall apart. We get sick, our daughters get pregnant, our cars go on the blink if not kept in sync, we make bad investments, our children turn to drugs, our dog dies, our homes go into foreclosure, our cars get repossessed, and we sometimes live in a deteriorated neighborhood. When these things happen too frequently, we generally end up back on square-one.

Life is also generally a zero-based proposition, and we lose the game based on attrition. And no matter how hard you try to survive, absolutely no one can gets out of it alive.

Life is hell. Then you die.

SOME LIFE-LONG TIPS

You didn't ask to come here, but yet you can't leave under your own terms.

Sometimes the people who brought you into this world don't like you either.

If your mother and father, indeed, knew everything about your life, they wouldn't like you either.

We get paranoid that other people don't like us, but most of the time other people couldn't care one way or the other.

We spend a lifetime trying to please other people, when most of them couldn't care less about what we do or say.

The individuals closest to us are the ones who betray us; because, we generally expect such behavior from people outside our circle.

Life is a zero-sum game in which the gravity of life will sometimes land us back on square-one.

Part of the satisfaction in life comes from not being able to predict what will happen tomorrow. If you could predict the future it would take all the fun and spontaneity out of life.

A bad attitude has never caused anyone to be a success. It's your attitude that determines your altitude. Having a loving, kind, and respectful attitude will take you a long way in this world.

Be independent; don't let other people determine your mode of behavior.

You are the highest creation of the Almighty God's imagination. Carry yourself in this regard.

Never go to bed with your anger, and never let the sun catch you crying.

There are gravitation-like social, economic, political, psychological, and educational forces in society that conspire to pull us down. We must learn to control these forces. The same as a pilot is able to overcome the G-Forces when flying a plane.

Be the best at what you do. If you are a dog catcher, be the best dog catcher there has ever been.

No job should be considered a dead-end job. See every job as a possible situation from which to get promoted—and a possible launching pad.

The only reason to give up is when you have explored every possible alternative, and found your resources are too limited for the situation.

Don't be a big pretender: know when to hold'em, when to fold'em, when to walk away, and when to run.

People generally do better if they know better. If nobody ever told you better, then I guess you don't know any better.

Don't sit around worried about what you don't have; take what you've got and make the best of it.

God helps those who help themselves. If you believe in yourself and God, and are aggressive in going after what you want, your wildest dreams will come true.

Prayer only helps you to focus on what you want, and when you focus on what you want, you will more aggressively go after it.

God has a specific plan for your life, if he didn't, you wouldn't still be here, and you would have been canned. What God has for you is only for you: you are one of a kind, God designed you with that in mind.

Don't try to move up until you've mastered where you are, and when you do move up, always give something back.

Live the life God intended for you to live, and be the person God intended for you to be.

PART III

FAMILY

WHY NOT BE A CONTINUOUS FOOL?

All my life I've been something of a fool:

I was a fool for plowing a mule on the farm from eleven years of age until eighteen years of age, on a dirt farm that was mostly rock, instead of figuring out a way to get off that farm and better my life.

I was a fool for attending a substandard elementary, junior high, and high school; instead of figuring out a way to attend a better school.

I was a fool for attending an integrated university, instead of attending a Historically Black one, where I might have been able to pick up some more of the basics that I didn't get in my primary education.

I was a fool for choosing a job in a state with a higher standard of living, where the salary was slightly higher, rather than taking a lower salary where I was living at the time.

I was a fool for leaving a decent job for one that had less promise.

I was a fool for buying a different house when the one I lived in was sufficient.

If I can do these things, when things go wrong in my family, why not be a continuous fool for my family—if necessary.

MARCUS

I had two sons; Marcus was my first born. For him, I have never had any regrets, or never been upset.

He has always been independent; always with a sense of his own conscience. Went to high school without any major issues. That was in line with his mother and my wishes.

He went to college and trade school, then went to New York on his own, and rarely bothered us, even by phone. Then he said he was leaving New York for California, that he had a better job offer, and was moving alone.

He has worked in California for many years. I will always hold him dear. Although, he rarely calls us on the phone, I'm happy that he can make it on his own. Boys are known for that type of song.

MARTIN

Martin was the youngest of my sons. Never gave me any major problems. What he presented it didn't take much to solve them.

He graduated college after a lot of hard work, and finally deciding what he wanted to do with his life. Some of us have a hard time just finding "us."

I hope he will land a good job; that is what all of us wish for our children—real hard.

Though he is twenty-seven, he is still my child, and I love him as if he were eleven.

Good luck; and I wish you well in your career. You are the greatest.

MY FRIEND

An older friend lived in a small Gulf Coast town. I met him while on vacation when I was six; I had few occasions to get out of the sticks.

My father worked in this town, a long way from home. My father took me on this much-needed vacation, and it was a cause for much elation.

We lived in a rural East Texas, on a farm, that caused all of us much harm. We were isolated with only a trail; we didn't even have access to our own mail.

My friend was strong and tall, and thought he had it all. He taught me about city living; said he didn't mind giving. He was self-assured and confident and knew how to take a compliment.

I'm sure my father paid him to take care of me and look after, because I was a walking disaster. My friend was fully capable of doing so, he was almost six-foot-four.

He was big and strong, and had been that way for his life-long. He took good care of me for those two weeks, and he never tried to preach.

He showed me around the city, and said that because I couldn't stay there and go to school was a pity. Tried to show me how to fight and when to take flight. Showed me the nitty-gritty of being able to survive in the city.

I went home after those two weeks, and was a better man because of what he had to teach, and again, he never attempted to preach. He was a good teacher, knew what he was doing, this time in the city help to keep me from ruin.

FRANCES

I met my wife in college, and we hit it off well. I knew she was special—even then.

We got married several years later, and have been together for forty-six special years. She is one of the few people on earth that I can say I truly love, regardless of how she feels, my love is unconditional for her.

We have had some ups and downs and crazy turn arounds, but we are still going, like the energizer bunny rabbit.

I hope we can make it until the other passes away. She is the most amazing human being I have ever known. With all her faults and shortcomings, she is still the greatest. I hope we can live together until the end of time.

But no one lives until the end of time. In that case, a ripe old age will be enough.

PART IV

THE ENVIRONMENT

MY EARLIEST
REMEMBRANCE

I was walking through a corn field in May. My brother was plowing the furrows. It felt good to my toes. I was bare feet and happy to be alive. I had no notions about stress or strife.

There were pretty azaleas planted in the yard. The pretty flowers distorted the fact that life was very hard. We had no electricity, gas, telephones or plumbing. All our messages came by drumming.

The chickens, the pigs, the dogs, the ducks, the guinea fowls, all left their droppings in the yard. If you did survive you would be scarred.

All I knew at the time was my sisters, brothers, father, and mother. What existed in the outside world, I had yet to discover.

I hadn't yet acquired any daily chores; at this point I only had to keep my own scores. But I had to grow older, and as I did, life would get colder.

THE DIRT ROAD

We didn't get a constructed dirt road until I was seven. But in my isolation, I didn't know hell from Heaven. I thought life was as good to me as it could possibly be.

I walked that dirt road to school every day. I was hoping to one day get a taste of the American way. It was a three-mile hike, both ways, and I made it most days.

Some days it was hot and dusty, and other days it was muddy and rusty. Some days I had to fight, and other days I had to take flight, but I made it.

My family didn't seem concerned; thought one day I would learn. The next year the bus picked us up at our front door, and the driver said we didn't have to walk to the bus stop any more.

I was happy I didn't have to any longer muddy my shoes, or get the walking blues, but I made it.

The road was uneven in places, and deep sand in others. I once got stuck on a rainy day while transporting my mother.

It took several people to push the car from the clutches of the mud. It was knee deep in sludge.

Soon after that they blacktopped the road, but it must not have been up to code, because it wore off after bearing many heavy loads. Once again, we were back to a three-mile dirt road.

The county didn't see fit to keep the blacktop repaired. Too many non-voters, but someone had to be spared. I guess we were the logical choice.

I left after high school as soon as I could. I had different concerns on my mind at the time. When I returned the road was still bare, and there was no one to care.

Years later it was much the same; as if the residents still hadn't learned the game. I hear now some new people have moved in, and not to keep the road up would be a sin.

THE THREE-MILE TRAIL

Until I was seven, we had nothing but a three-mile trail to our house. The trail led off a winding highway that led to small towns in either direction.

The trail was narrow with trees hugging the trail. In some places, ditches were as deep as a house. A wagon could barely navigate the trail; and it was best done on foot or horseback.

When it rained the area became a flood plain, and one could barely get through the area. My father eventually left for the Gulf Coast, and my sisters and brothers moved away.

My sisters and brothers created many stories about ghost and goblins lurking along the trail, and created many stories about wild animals along the trail. No one in my family would dare travel at night because of these stories.

When I was seven-years-old the county built a dirt road that made traveling easier. It decreased our isolation, and we all took a breather.

THE CRADLE CAFÉ

The Cradle Café sat in the middle of town. It was the only café around. Mold and mildew were all over the walls—much like the horses' stalls. I would sit there for hours at a time; just as if I was blind.

The café wasn't integrated, and the races had to be segregated. This was in 1965; it was a time when none of us were quite alive. The furniture in the Black section was broken down, much like everything else around.

One night my cousin and I attempted to desegregate. We got tired of the way things were, and wanted to see what could occur. We walked through that precious gate. But the proprietor paid us no attention, and things went on without mention.

I think the Cradle Café eventually went out of business rather than make the right decision. I at some point left town and never returned to see what was around. A friend told me many years later that the Cradle Café had been torn down.

I hope the overall atmosphere in that town has changed, and that the attitude of the Cradle Café will never rise again.

STABBING AT THE CRADLE CAFÉ

My sister worked at the Cradle Café as a waitress. It was twenty miles away. I would drive her there every single day.

It wasn't known for fights, even if there were sometimes obvious slights. Usually these friendly slights were between friends, who had no real intent of changing the trend.

One night two fools came in who had been getting on each other's nerves. One thought the other had thrown him a curve.

One said to the other, "Why were you hugging on my girl?" The other one said, "I didn't know she was your special pearl."

The one pulled out a knife and stuck it in the other guy's arm as fast as lightening. It was a little bit frightening.

The one guy stood there staring at the six-inch blade sticking out of his arm, much as if it was some kind of charm.

The other guy ran off into the night. He had carried out his plight.

I sat there until I could stand no more, and eventually headed for the door.

I don't know if such incidents were common for the café, or if such was par for the array. From that point on I made my visits to the Cradle only occasional.

THE REGAL
BLACK STUD

The regal black stud mounts a submissive sometimes partially resisting mare. If she didn't desire it, he could not mount her at all.

He is regal, majestic, and black. It seems bestial the way he mounts her, but it is not cruel or unusual punishment. It is in keeping with the Almighty's plan for continuing the species.

Afterwards, they run off to the pasture, playful and completely satisfied, having done what nature intended for them to do.

THE CHURCH
AND RELIGION

The only book in our precious house was the Bible, and maybe a dogeared copy of *Paradise Lost*. Until I was eleven years of age my mother made her way through the grassy fields, with ticks and red bugs, and made her way to the Sunday spiel.

When I was still eleven, my brother left an old 1951 Chevrolet parked in an old dilapidated shed next to the house—I was in Heaven. He began to teach me how to drive before he left.

I would then get in the car and go-go-go. The more I drove I only wanted more. Soon I began to take my mother to church, and she then used me as a kind of crutch. My brother had left for the Gulf Coast, said he dug it the most.

The church sat on a red-dirt road—near the end of that road—those who lived there carried a heavy load. It was unpainted, with a rusty-tin roof, and those who worshipped were very aloof.

It had pews made of rough-hewn pine wood that had splinters, and they would grab and tear your clothes in a hot second—this wasn't difficult to reckon. It was heated by a potbellied stove, and you had to wear plenty of clothes.

There was no air conditioning—this would soon lead to attrition. It was cold during the winter and too hot during the summer—that was quite a bummer. We had a lay minister that seemed jealous of any qualified preacher—not a good quality in a teacher.

We had no Christmas or Easter services for the youth. I was the only young person that attended the church, and I was only there to transport my mother—because she deserved it. We had no Bible study or Vacation Bible School. We only met each Sunday for a minute—as a rule.

My mother was religious and spiritual; she felt that for God to take care of her was critical. She kept praying, believing, wishing, and hoping that this God was not doping.

I don't believe she ever saw any benefit from her believing. She did live a full life without excessive grieving.

She did live to be eighty-nine-years old—that was like finding a pot of gold. I suppose that's a blessing in itself. This blessing was all she had left.

Once a member of the church said that the Church of Christ was the only true church, primarily because the church was named after Christ Himself, and you had to believe it or you would miss much.

I argued with several classmates about the idea that the Church of Christ was the only true church (Word). They called me an idiot, and told me not to believe everything I heard. I walked away feeling like a nerd.

My mother and brother once had a discussion over whether God was Black or white—or just light. They couldn't reach any definite conclusions, but only added to the general confusion. I was left to reach my own conclusion about religion.

In the first place I have concluded that all religions are created by man. All societies have come up with their own ideas about religion according to the dictates of their culture and their preceding cascades. There has been no society on record that didn't develop concepts about religion and how it has played.

The God of the Bible was made up by man, and if there is a true God, the God of the Bible is no where close to the real plan. Man is finite and God is infinite, therefore man will never be able to fully conceive the true God.

WHAT I LIKED ABOUT RURAL EAST TEXAS

There was good fishing, good hunting, and it was wild and free country.

One could grow up without being influenced by gangs or drugs.

Schools were inadequate for mainstream society, but taught some of the basics.

You could drive for miles without worrying about being stopped by the police.

We grew our own food, raised our own animals, and thus had plenty to eat.

We were close but yet so far from larger cities.

You could roam the country side for as much and as long as you wanted with no one to bother you.

You had time to do a lot of uninterrupted thinking.

You weren't under the close scrutiny of anyone.

The forest, the hills, and the valleys, and plenty of sunshine.

The friendly people. They were polite and would give you the shirt off their backs.

The people lived for apart from one another.

WHAT I DIDN'T
LIKE ABOUT RURAL
EAST TEXAS

The hard work on the farm.

The difficulty in getting from one place to another.

The inadequate school system.

The extreme isolation at an early age.

The ticks, red bugs, fleas, and the numerous snakes.

The fact that we didn't have proper equipment for managing a modern farm.

Inadequate availability of jobs.

Lacks of wholesome activities to engage in.

The fact that my parents had a slave and sharecropper's mentality.

The fact that my parents refused to give up on the farm; even though working it had outlived its practicality.

PART V

PERSONAL ISSUES

PIGTAILS AND A DRESS

My mother dressed me in pigtails and a dress until I was three years of age; never considering what would be written on my page.

She was from the old school, and had some damn tough rules. She would take a hickory stick to your back; never considering the consequences of her act.

We lived far off the beaten path; too far to be considered part of the census track. My mother didn't think much of dressing me in pigtails and a dress; said she would answer to her Savior, and there was nothing wrong with her behavior.

She never came to my school, and decided on her own rules. Never had a course in human behavior, and said that no one could question her but her Savior.

Few people saw me in those pigtails and that dress, no one but family, if they had it might have been cause for some distress.

I was successful in life, depending on how you measure success, and depending on how you measure strife.

I left those woods and never looked back; I was determined to improve my act. I'm sure that dress and pigtails are still having some effect on me, but I want let it have a major effect on how I be.

A HUMAN/ANIMAL

My mother turned me loose with the other domesticated animals as soon as I was out of diapers, also to deal with the vipers. There were wolves, coyotes, and others just to name a few, but usually they didn't bother you.

I spent most of my time with the animals; didn't have time to read the manual. I developed some animal instincts; my human behavior went on the blink.

I was much like a coyote: always nervous and quick to revolt. Always on the run like a hungry bum.

I still didn't read much in high school, but did get to college, so I did get a little knowledge. In the end I guess I still have some of my old animal instincts.

IT'S A GOOD
DAY TO DIE

In high school I was young and didn't know what was going on—we didn't even have a phone. But I was trying to court, yet I was naïve at the sport.

One young man had observed me and my girl for a while, and decided he would impose himself on my style. He approached me and my girl one sunny day. He decided it was time for him to prey.

Said he was taking over my girl. He was going to make her his special pearl. I responded with outrage, and came out of my cage. I responded to his lust with disgust.

"What do you mean?" I asked, "You want to take my girl for a whirl?" He was popular, and had had many rehearsals; I was immature and demure.

He said, "Give me a chance at romance. I'm sure I can make her my girl, and we can do this dance, if you will only give us a chance." My girl said, "I have to decided which one I want." I didn't realize it was a game, my notion of life was too plain.

I also didn't realize that when a man tries to move in on you simply because he wants to, lock, stock, and barrel, then "It's a good day to die," no matter what stage of life you're in.

A LESSON WELL LEARNED

I was only six years of age, never had strife in my life, beyond that of normal country living. My father thought he would be giving, and invited me to try city living.

He worked away from home, three-hundred miles away on the coast, decided he liked that the most. He was taking me on vacation for a few weeks. I guess he noticed my depravity.

My father introduced me to one of his friend's sons; he was going to show me the run. One day we went to the community center to play some pool, and maybe some Ping-Pong, and I learned a different song.

He signed us up to play pool; he was going to take me to school. I was young and never played before; how was I to know the score. My friend picked up his cue, and that's the day I grew to rue. The other guy said it was his turn. Things then went to ruin.

My friend said, "How dare you brother, try to walk in on me, I think you had better let me be." Before the guy knew what was happening, my friend had hit him in the jaw. The guy was on the floor before I saw.

My friend left and ran away, and I had to answer the fray. I learned never to be violent. It wasn't meant to be that way. I eventually went back to the country after two weeks. But I had learned to never be violent unless completely necessary.

ANY DAY IS A
GOOD DAY TO DIE

Any day is a good day to die when:

When you or your family members' lives are threatened.

When someone imposes themselves on you in a forceful manner against your will.

When you are called to fight for your country.

When someone demonstrates an obvious attempt to take what belongs to you.

When someone tries to take advantage of someone obviously not able to defend themselves.

When anyone tries to take another individual's life.

Whenever there is no alternative but death.

Whenever God decides that your time is up.

In considering whether any day is a good day to die, we must all use discernment, good judgment is important to your decision.

JOHNNY AND I

Johnny and I would roam the hills every day, it was our only form of play; we never stopped to play cards, throw a baseball, or catch a football. We weren't concerned about getting played; we wanted to get paid and get laid.

I didn't have much time for play, but wished I could every day. When we got a chance, we would hit the road, trying to unburden ourselves of our heavy load.

Sometimes we would walk for miles; just happy to be young bucks—wild and with at least two smiles. Johnny was different than me, he didn't have farm work, so he was free.

I must say that most of our times in those days were good to the extent that you think they could.

There came a time when both of us went our own way; neither of us had much to say. We knew it would eventually end; when we came to a bend.

I went off to college to get some knowledge. I didn't figure Johnny would make it through high school. After I graduated high school, he had two more years left. My talks to him had only been good for the deaf.

I learned Johnny died in that same shack, and I never ventured to look back.

SEAN

Sean put forth a demeanor like a Doberman pinscher, but was really more like a French poodle. He also overestimated his academic abilities, and when it came to knowledge was non-porous like a water lily.

Sean came from a decent background, but in plain terms hadn't mastered his nouns. He would put on airs, but you could see he had many tears.

We found it hard to get along, but neither of us could figure out what was wrong. Our personalities just didn't blend, and our attitudes couldn't mend.

In the Army, he wore my new blazer without my knowledge, and burned a big hole right in the sleeve. Didn't even apologize or grieve. Then he took my mother's homemade quilt to lay in the mud with some sleaze.

One day we just gave up on one another, and said we couldn't make it another further. I never regretted ending our friendship to this day. Incompatibility in a friendship at some point is bound to lead to decay.

DYING A LITTLE EVERY DAY

We all die a little every day:

I died a little when I was born.

I died a little when my family failed to provide the necessary attention, affection, and support.

I died a little when my mother dressed me in my sister's hand-me-down dresses until I was three years of age.

I died a little after being neglected during my formative years in school.

I died a little when my mother insisted that I wear my sister's old hand-me-down coat to school on one cold day in December. For some reason I didn't have a coat. I don't remember the circumstances.

I died a little when one of my teachers slapped me as if I was a grown man.

I died a little when some of my elementary teachers neglected their classes.

And I die a little after further neglect in high school.

I died a little when schizophrenia began to occur in my family.

I died a little when I developed paranoid schizophrenia.

Fortunately, any other neglect or abuse can only be attributed to my own personal fault. But one dies a little every day from abuse and neglect. But I'm still here—alive and kicking.

BETTER SOLDIER
AS AN OFFICIER

The military has supported me for most of my life. The only thing I can say about it is I would have made a better officer than an enlisted man. I was willing to fight and die for my country in whatever way I had to.

I went in the military for somewhat of a selfish reason. At the time I had no other way of taking care of myself. In my life it was a bad season.

I had spent my last penny trying to survive college. My sole ambition was to acquire some knowledge. I left college with no place to go but back home.

My family couldn't help me. So, I joined the military, but I knew this was only being contrary. I was hoping to become an officer, but became an enlisted man instead. It was all I could git, and it was too late to resist.

My background hadn't prepared me on every hand, but still I could have been a better officer than an enlisted man. I had some rough spots sure enough, but most men have some spots that are rough. I feel I could have better adjusted to an officer's plan rather than being an enlisted man.

Don't get me wrong, I'm grateful for how the military help to make me strong. It helped me beyond the average man's comprehension. But still feel I could have been more in the plan if I had been an officer rather than an enlisted man.

My education didn't prepare me to take orders, but prepared me to give them. I continue to feel I could have held a better hand, been grand, if I only had been an officer rather than an enlisted man.

A PERFECT
DAY TO DIE

The Native Americans said, "It's a good day to die." That was their mantra. When a man tries to take what rightfully belongs to you there is no other contra.

The Native Americans believed it is what God intended; and there is no other way to suspend it. They also believed they should be ready to die on any given day, and this should take place any given day the Almighty God might say.

You can bet the Native Americans would die with no regrets. This was their culture, and they had no intentions of yielding to any vultures. That's why they believed it was important to begin each day fresh; it was the only way they and their culture could mesh.

The Indians didn't let past distractions interfere with their interactions with the Almighty God.

PERSONALITY
AND PARANOIA

My mother and father didn't like me, and they took every opportunity to strike me.

My sisters and brothers didn't like me, and they did everything to spite me.

My relatives didn't like me, and they tried to fight me.

The people in my community didn't like me, and they kept their distance.

My girlfriend didn't like me, and she wouldn't be good to me.

Some of my teachers didn't like me, and they failed to educate me properly.

The people at college didn't like me, and they spread rumors about me.

The people on my jobs didn't like me, and they failed to be supportive.

People in general don't seem to like me, and they have an attitude about me.

Sometimes I don't think my wife likes me either, but she married me, she must have liked me to some degree.

TO LIVE IN PEACE

I have lived a good-long life, but not one free from strife. I don't here want to talk about my earlier years, but only the life I have yet to live.

I have two good sons, a good wife, a nice house, and peace of mind, that is something to go down in time. My health is fair and I have decent transportation, and I believe all these things are worthy of an oration.

I am retired and living a life of ease—if you please. To live long and healthy is something I never expected; though, I don't think a monument to me will ever be erected.

I am seventy-two-years old, and still somewhat bold, though I'm not in complete control. If I had an Aladdin lamp, I wouldn't even make a change, I am happy with the way I have played the game.

I'm going to keep living, the way I have always done, in accordance with where I come from. If I never amass a great fortune, I'm happy with my life without excessive distortion.

PART VI

EDUCATION

STARTING SCHOOL

I was late starting school, and didn't know some of the familiar rules: like colors, geometric shapes, letters, or numbers, and I didn't even know how to fight or rumble.

My parents nor my sisters and brothers had prepared me for an intense game, and I must admit I was sort of lame. I started when the next month I would be seven; had no preschool, kindergarten, or daycare; and from where I came nobody knew where.

My teacher was good; she understood. She was a neighbor who was conversant with people who had experienced my type of labor. I learned what I could, but knew I was behind the eight ball, trying to play catch up, and felt I would never be able to match up.

I kept trying, my teachers passed me on, even though I had never heard of a "king-on-the-throne." My background left me with a certain lacuna. I had some holes that weren't obvious to the naked eye.

COTTON PICKING

One year my brother suggested, "Instead of going back to school, lets go out west and pick cotton." We were living in East Texas and used to being on the bottom.

Out west was a rich-cotton farming area near Dallas. It was no palace. I hesitated for a few seconds and thought about it for a long while, but finally agreed to go, even though it was against my style.

My brother had graduated high school, but like many others still couldn't conform to the rules. He considered going out west to pick cotton was panning for gold in California in 1949, and would definitely give him time and peace of mind.

There were several other high school graduates, dropouts, and some still in high school; but few of them had mastered the rules.

My mother and brother agreed that picking some cotton may be worthwhile, and I finally agreed to go. Why I did it I will never know. My mother was for anything that meant less school and more work; after all picking cotton was designed for jerks.

So, we got on the road. It was an open bobtail truck. The wind on the trip ran us amuck. Soon we arrived at our destination. The trip was uneventful, and I was unable to be resentful.

The dirt in the area was rich and black, unlike the clay and sand in East Texas. I thought about hurling several invectives, realizing at that point I couldn't correct it.

We lived in a cotton pickers shack, and conveniences were slack. We all slept on the floor on several matts gathered together. We had no privacy, and there was no telephone, bathtub, or shower. We had to improvise from hour to hour.

I picked 200 lbs. a day. That was four dollars earned by the way. The sun bored down on us in the September season. It came on us without reason. We were pulling rather than picking cotton. I couldn't afford gloves, and the prickly-dried cotton bow would stick into my fingers. For this I was not a dead ringer.

Lunch consisted of bologna, mayonnaise, bread, and a cold drink of some kind. It was definitely hard on the mind. One day I said I wanted to return home, and they all agreed I had probably had enough.

They all did laugh and said, "Go home?" They thought I was silly, and said, "You just got here." But I think the proprietor felt sorry for me and took me home. After all, slavery had ended with the Emancipation Proclamation. Some of the other guys wanted to go home for the annual county fair.

I went home that weekend. That put going out west to pick cotton to an end. I went to the county fair, and it felt good to be home and take in some of that East Texas fresh air.

On Monday morning I was back in school. My objective was to gain knowledge and understand the Golden Rule. Since that time, I have always valued long-term educational gain over short-term economic gain.

HIGH SCHOOL

High school was good; learned as much as I could. But I was plagued with thoughts earlier inculcated in me about just doing enough to get by; usually I wouldn't even try. I felt you were smart if you did as little as you possibly could.

The smartest thing I felt I could do was to avoid exerting any energy toward school. I know at this point that sounds like such a jerk. But something happened to me which made me try harder. I guess I realized on this road I was going to need something with which to barter.

I made the third highest ACT score in my class of those who took the test, and was ranked number three out of a class of eighty. Somehow, I had managed to come back quick and steady.

I went on to college seeking greater knowledge. Knew I had a better chance than some who had taken a different stance.

OUR HIGH SCHOOL SENIOR TRIP

For our high school senior trip, we took an excursion to Houston. I don't remember all the places we visited; but I do remember visiting Texas Southern University, Herman Park Zoo, and the San Jacinto Monument.

The trip was uneventful until we got back more than half way. We were in Nacogdoches, Texas, about eighty miles from Marshall, Texas, having gone most of the way, as they say.

I said as soon as we passed this particular college, "That's the school I will attend for college," very proudly. My friend and I were sitting on the same seat trying to beat the heat. It was early May in East Texas and the sun was beaming down. The young lady was positioned and sandwiched between us like a piece of meat on two slices of wonder bread. The bus was not air conditioned.

My friend replied, "You can't go to college, you can't write." I knew that was out of sight. I didn't know if he was saying, my cursive writing was unintelligible, or my grammar and syntax needed some work. But he was right in both regards, and I did not take it too hard.

As I usually did in such situations, I didn't suffer any degradation. If I considered what an individual said was logical and within reason, I moved on to another season.

What he didn't say was that my teachers had not been much help in speeding me along my way. They never showed me how to form my letters, or taught me proper grammar or syntax, that didn't make things any better. This was true in elementary, junior high, and high school. But we didn't keep talking on the subject, and focused our attention on other objects.

We made the young lady sitting between us the nucleus of our attention. We both began to kiss her. She allowed both of us to indulge and then seem to have a grudge. She told the principal I had encroached upon her and reproached her.

The principal was outraged; said he thought I was a sage. He said he would take action against this infraction. I told him my friend had also did the same thing. But he wasn't phased by my plea, and said that he didn't look upon my actions with glee.

He became mute and acted astute. My guess is if my friend hadn't done the same thing, he might have considered sending me to Sing Sing. But he did allow me to graduate, and that made me sate.

COLLEGE

I went to college and found myself a stranger in a strange land. But much like many others on the other hand. I wasn't prepared in some ways, but in others I had had some productive days.

I hadn't read much, but had listened very carefully. Outside readings were done in high school rarely. So, I listened, read, and studied as much as I could, knowing that if a man with my background could graduate, then I surely would.

I didn't know how to choose a college to attend. So, I ended up being on the mend. I wanted to do something for integration, it was the days of civil rights, and everyone was seemingly uptight.

So, I chose a state school that was close to home, in that way to get home I wouldn't have to take out another school loan. And on holidays, when the dorms closed, I wouldn't be completely out on my nose.

One day I was able to walk across the stage and was graduated. It wasn't the degree I wanted, but at least I had matriculated.

I was one of the first Black students to get a degree; there were a few others before me. I graduated with a "B" average and felt kind of savvy. But I was still lost, and hadn't taken time to count the cost.

I graduate with no job and no plans. I thought after graduating I would be half ready to meet the man. So, I became steadfast, and took a stand. I would go into the military until I could develop a better hand.

GET A GOOD
EDUCATION AND
GET A GOOD JOB

I grew up in an isolated, rural, multi-problem family, and had my share of issues.

Struggled through primary and secondary school, while being neglected and abused, but they said, "Get a good education and get a good job."

Struggled through college, but they said, "Get a good education and get a good job."

Joined the military to try and see some of the world and broaden my horizon.

Attended two different graduate schools after the military, receiving degrees from both, and they reminded me, "Get a good education and get a good job."

Studied toward a Ph.D. at two different university programs, as they still uttered, "Get a good education and get a good job."

I did everything I knew how to be a red-blooded American boy.

My education and my socialization were deficient in some regards, but adequate in most respects. And I still had difficulty in finding a decent job. I was still only able to get the same jobs that many less qualified people were able to get.

ABOUT THE AUTHOR

JAY THOMAS WILLIS is a graduate of the University of Houston, Houston, Texas, where he earned a Masters' degree in social work; he is also a graduate of the Masters' degree counselling program at Texas Southern University, Houston, Texas. He attended undergraduate school at Stephen F. Austin State University, Nacogdoches, Texas, where he earned a B.S. degree in sociology and social and rehabilitative services.

He worked as a Clinical Social Worker for seventeen years, and provided direct clinical services as well as supervision. He has been a consultant to a nursing home and a boys' group home; taught college courses in sociology, family, and social work in community college and university settings; and has worked as a family therapist for several agencies in the Chicago area. In addition, he was a consultant to a number of home-health care agencies in the south suburbs and Chicago. Mr. Willis is a past CHAMPUS peer reviewer for the American Psychological Association and the American

Psychiatric Association. He also spent a number of years in private practice as a Licensed Clinical Social Worker in the State of Illinois.

Mr. Willis has traveled and lectured extensively on the condition of the African American community. He has written thirty-two books, and written many journal articles on the subject of the African American community. He has written several magazine articles. He has also written Op-Ed Commentaries for the *Chicago Defender, Final Call, East Side Daily News* of Cleveland, and *Dallas Examiner*. He currently lives in Richton Park, Illinois with his wife and son.

Printed in the United States
By Bookmasters